# My Awesome SHARKS BOOK

make
believe
ideas

# WHAT IS A SHARK?

Sharks are a type of fish that can be found in oceans all around the world.

great white shark

bonnethead shark

whale shark

Some can use their **tail** as a whip, look like **seaweed**, or even **walk** across coral!

Sharks are JAW-some!

blue shark

great hammerhead shark

# GREAT WHITE SHARK

Great white sharks are excellent hunters. They have around 300 razor-sharp teeth.

## HOW BIG?

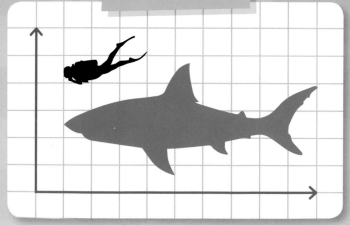

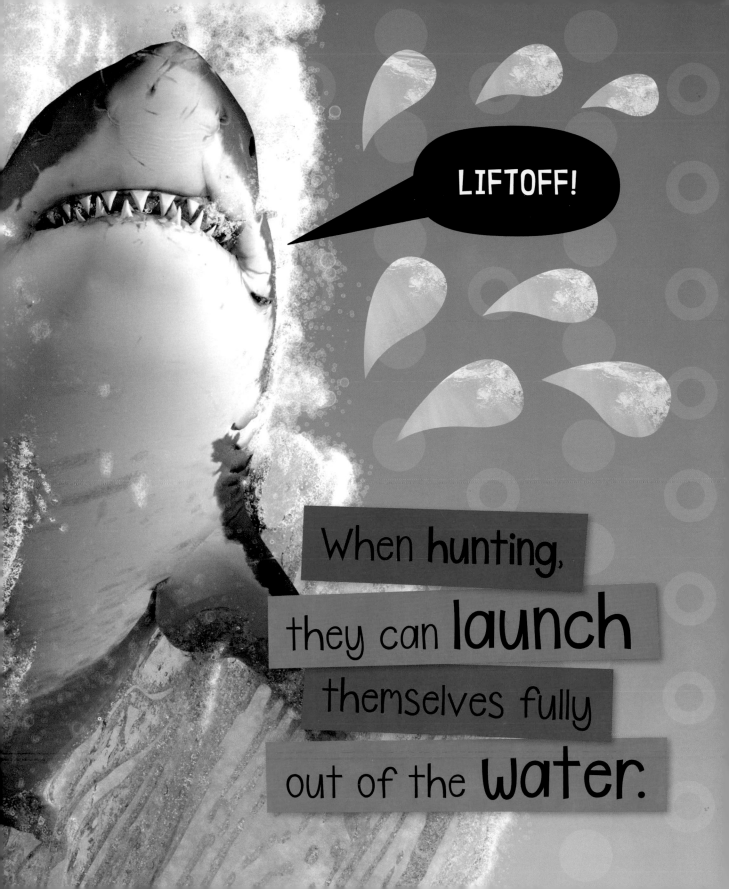

# HAMMERHEAD SHARK

There are eight different types of hammerhead shark. The great hammerhead shark is the largest, and the scalloped bonnethead shark is the smallest.

**NAILED it!**

## HOW BIG?

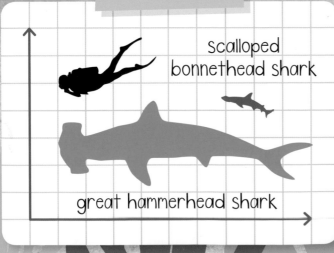

scalloped bonnethead shark

great hammerhead shark

## HOW BIG?

They have the **strongest** bite of all sharks.

# WHALE SHARK

Whale sharks are the largest fish in the oceans. They can grow as long as a bus!

I'm having a WHALE of a time!

They **gulp** down plankton and fish near the **surface** of the **ocean**.

HOW BIG?

# TIGER SHARK

Tiger sharks get their name from the dark stripes they have when they are young.

## HOW BIG?

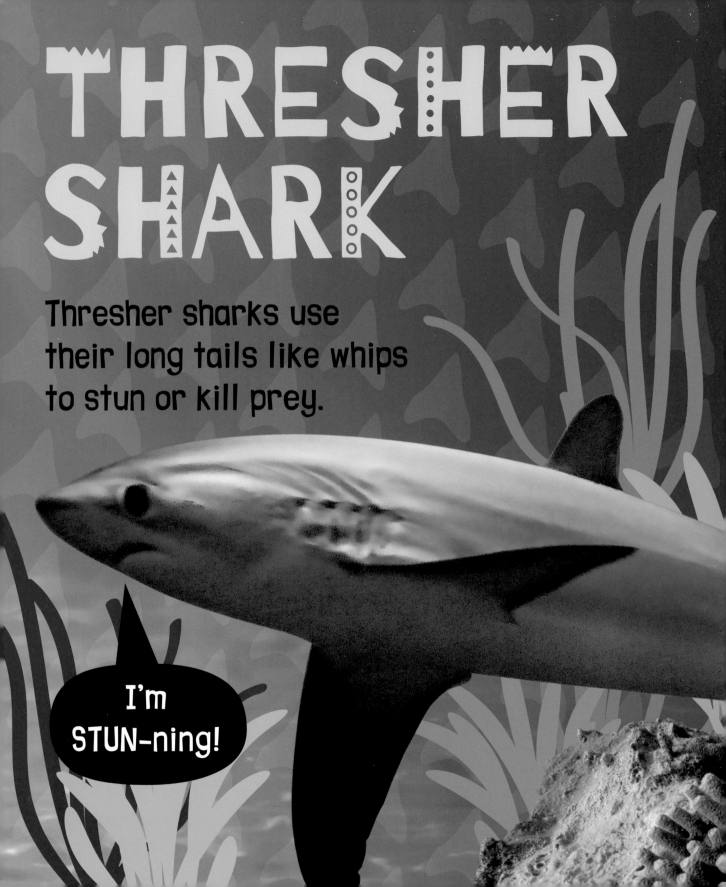

Their long **tails** are around the same **length** as their bodies!

**HOW BIG?**

# BLUE SHARK

Blue sharks move around in groups and will often gather together by age, or whether they are male or female.

HOW BIG?

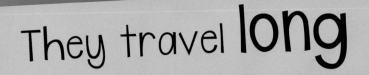

They travel **long** distances every year, around **5,600 miles** (9,000 km).

I love to **TRAVEL!**

# TASSELLED WOBBEGONG SHARK

Tasselled wobbegong sharks have frills around their mouths that look like seaweed. When a fish is near, they snap their jaws and catch their prey.

Their patterned, flat bodies are a perfect **disguise** as they rest on **coral reefs**.

# SWELL SHARK

Swell sharks can swallow a lot of water, which causes them to swell up to almost double their size. This makes it hard for predators to eat them.

## HOW BIG?

Their skin reflects the **moonlight**, so they look like they are glowing **bright** green.

GLOW for it!

# EPAULETTE SHARK

Epaulette sharks can walk across the coral and rocks using their fins like legs.

## HOW BIG?

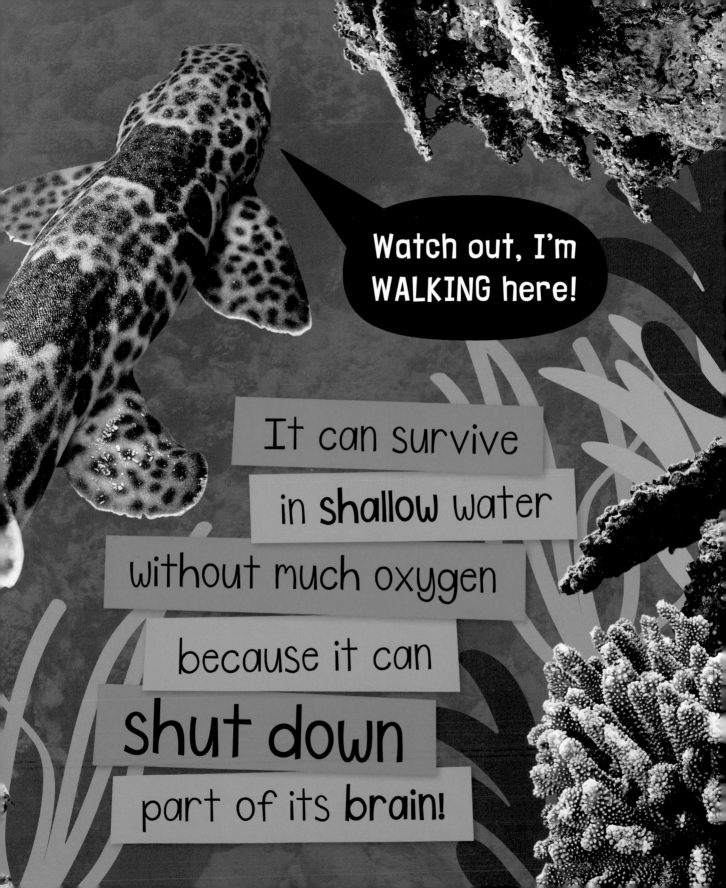

# BASKING SHARK

Basking sharks have hundreds of tiny teeth, but they don't use them! Instead, they open their mouths really wide and scoop up small animals called plankton.

Open WIDE!

## HOW BIG?

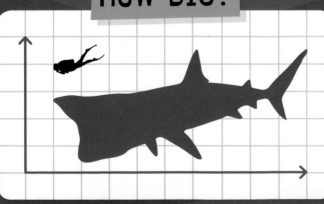

These gentle **giants** are the **second-largest** fish in the ocean!

# GREENLAND SHARK

Greenland sharks live in very cold water and swim really, really slowly – about as fast as you can walk!

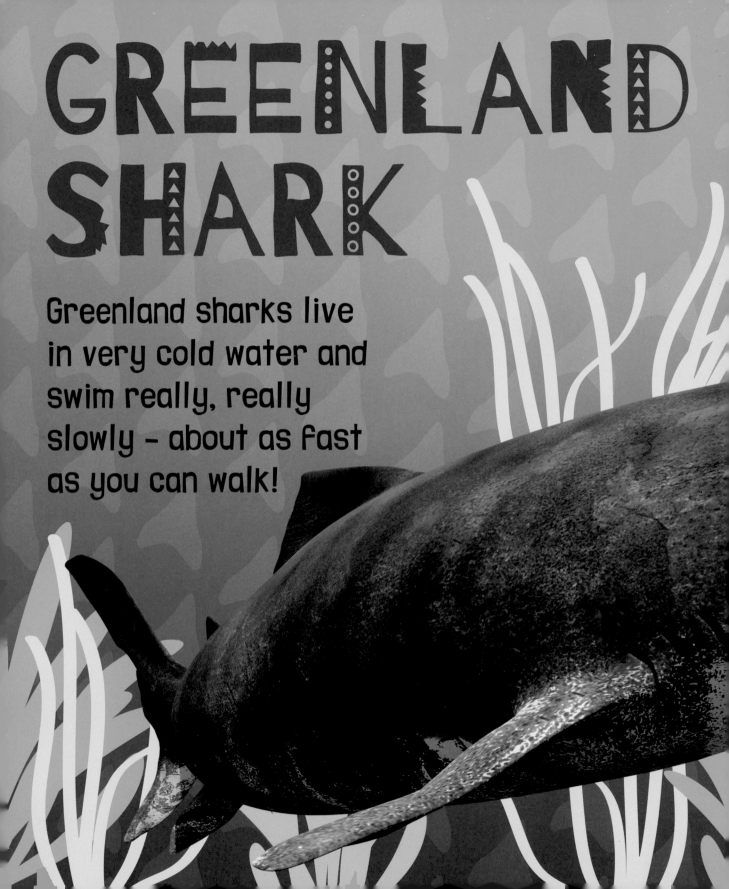

# SHORTFIN MAKO SHARK

Shortfin mako sharks are the fastest sharks. They can swim with short bursts of speed to catch their prey.

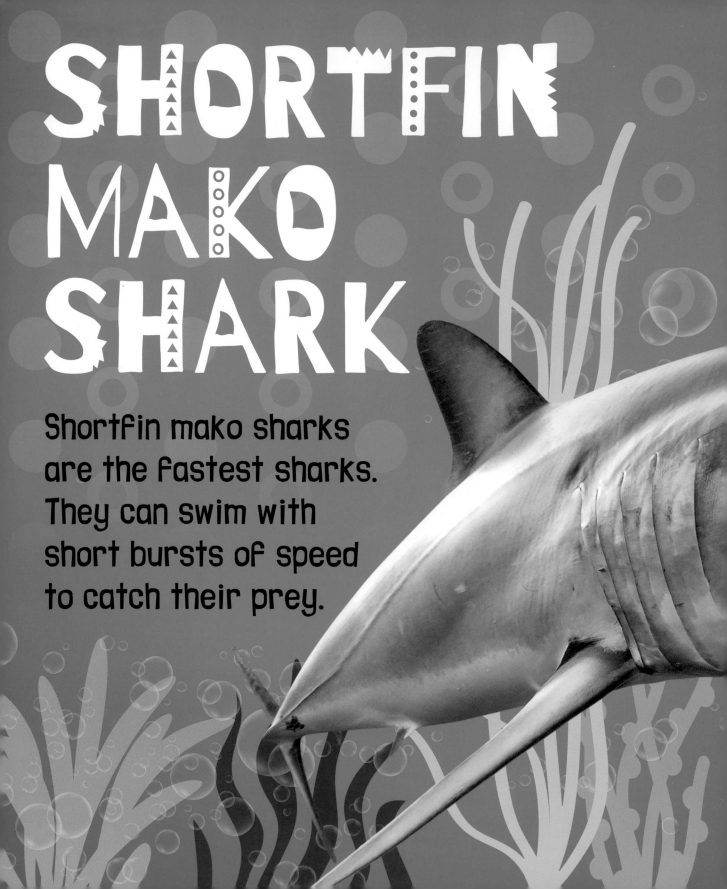

They hunt **fast-moving** prey, such as swordfish, tuna, and other **sharks.**

You **MAKO** me smile!

HOW BIG?

# MEGALODON

This fierce hunter became extinct about 3.6 million years ago. Scientists think that megalodon was the biggest shark that has ever lived.

HOW BIG?

megalodon

great white shark

I was
MEGA huge!

Its **mouth** was so **big**, a grown **man** could have stood up inside it!